Praise for
making noise

"A very enjoyable read from start to finish. I could hear Vilma's voice clearly in every poem. There's a gutsiness in the political poems, a bright singing in the poems about writing and creation, a rich solemnity in the poems that honor the memory of creators, poets, musicians, friends, and her own life's work—all part of the celebration reflected in the explosion of color and light chosen as an opening image for the collection. My personal favorites were 'f___ing [fleeting] expletives,' 'acoustic kitty,' 'visiting bee,' 'before words,' 'music manuscripts,' and 'solo recital.' I also really liked the phrase 'our covenant of quiet' from the poem 'silence revisited.' It so captures the resignation and complicity that has gotten us to this brink of indifferent, self-gratifying, soul-destroying capital-fascism."

—Terry Ehret, Sonoma County Poet Laureate, 2004–2005

"From 'speaking up' boldly and clearly, to 'word sounds' from her muse's murmurs, and to 'joyful noises,' jubilant *joyeux* with a hint of *tristesse*, section by section Vilma Ginzberg writes from age and outrage, from doubt and wisdom, and with gracious gratitude. *Making noise* joins Ginzberg's other superbly penned works to touch our shared human experience with the intimacy of a dearly-held friend."

—Ann Carranza, poet, reporter, videographer

"Thank God that octogenarian Vilma Ginzberg cannot help herself. She must 'make noise,' and once again does so insistently, angrily, touchingly, and beautifully in her latest poetry collection unsurprisingly titled *making noise*. Every poem that Ms. Ginzberg writes truly embodies the woman she is now, the product of her long life as a psychologist, activist, and all around feisty but loving human being. However, it's not enough for Vilma Ginzberg to look back and reflect on politics, sounds, loves, and music, she goes a step beyond and looks forward to her own death in the movingly provocative 'After the Funeral.' Read this book as a wise poet moves forward never missing a step."

—Ed Coletti, author of *When Hearts Outlive Minds* (2011) and *Germs, Viruses, and Catechisms* (Civil Defense Publications, San Francisco 2013)

"Vilma Ginzberg's collection of poems is music. While reading many of these poems—but especially her poems 'Rift Valley, Kenya' and 'after the goodbye' and, most especially, her birthday gift to me—'for Chester Aaron at 90'—I heard music—music I can only identify with reliance on the tribute Classical."

—Chester Aaron, author of 20-plus books, garlic-grower

making noise

making noise

new poems

Vilma Olsvary Ginzberg

McCaa Books • Santa Rosa

McCaa Books
1535 Farmers Lane #211
Santa Rosa, CA 95405-7535

Library of Congress Control Number: 2013933196

ISBN 978-0-9838892-7-4

First published in 2013 by McCaa Books,
an imprint of McCaa Publications.

Printed in the United States of America
Set in Tahoma

Author's photograph by Ann Carranza.

www.mccaabooks.com

For those who dare to speak out against injustice,
for those who actively practice the arts,
and for those not afraid to express gratitude,
my thanks.

Contents

speak up!

word-sounds

joyfulnoises

speak up!

a voice, n.   to voice, v.

silence revisited

(or: ode to my beloved country)

if you can't say something nice,
don't say nothin' at all

like the squatter morning glory vine
yielding pink and purple posies of promise
our bitter silence sends out relentless tendril roots
invading every corner of serenity's garden

silence is golden

rings of silence as daunting as barbed wire
imprison both sides

with shroud of silence
shall we cover the unflattering nakedness
of our outrage
while, masquerading as the cloak of civility,
our stillness, whether soft or steely,
is finally buried with us in mass graves of apathy
with no other companion
than our covenant of quiet?

make noise
make every day new year's eve,
clattering on the brink
of something hopeful

make noise
like the women taking back the night
like the bonus army insisting on their due
say your piece
like rachel carson martin luther king mahatma ghandi
pete seeger dmitri shostakovitch lenore kandel
mort sahl george carlin deep throat
project censored the wisconsin 14
like all the unnamed truth-tellers

like the canary in the coal-mine
sing as if your life depends on it

a spill of words

this is no New York Times Sunday crossword puzzle

these word games are much more serious
        ...spell that *"d.e.a.d.l.y"*

this is no little child's accident
no small finite milk *"spill"*
        from a container   onto a countertop
so easily wiped up with a paper towel
        the surface left pristine   unblemished

do not believe the lies they spew
        with their carefully crafted word games

this is a *hemorrhage*
        caused by incompetent surgeons
                making careless incisions
        beneath our cool blue watery skin
        through the muscle of ocean floor
        into this fragile planet's sensitive innards

this is a *hemorrhage* of aortic proportions
        ...call it by its name

because they have no tourniquets for the *hemorrhage*
        no surgical thread
                no close-the-wound training
they bring us paper towels of language
        to clean up their *"spill"* of words
hoping we won't see the truth

do not let them get away with their word games
        about the state of our precious Mother's body

refuse to call it a *"spill"*
refuse to let them call it a mere *"spill"*

it is a *hemorrhage*
it is an aortic *hemorrhage*
        of life-threatening proportion
it may be bleeding us to death

f___ing [fleeting] **expletives**

while agrichem CEOs poison our farms our rivers our bees
our very body-cells for their bottom line

and pharmaceutical actuaries collect our insurance lottery
premiums ransom our health reject high-risk losers
for their bottom line

and our precious suffrage is compromised in mysterious ways
for whose bottom line?

our august court of supreme justice
having nothing better to do in these lazy days
of snowboarding, no watersurfing, no waterboarding
our highest court of justice
because it is the true decider trusted defender of our freedoms
has opted to take on for deliberation the profound ethical
problem of "fleeting expletives"
...I'm not f___ing [fooling] with you...
one example of which is the surprised oscar winner exclaiming
on live tv *this is so f__ing cool!*

only heaven can know for sure
but pardon my imagining how dauntingly difficult it must be
what a high calling to monitor the spontaneous excitements
of 300 million faulted human beings
to protect our innocent ears from such "fleeting expletives"

nonetheless it being their mission they say
endowed by our f___ing [founding] fathers
to protect us from the f___ings [failings] of society
they are this day taking this f___ing [fledgling] issue
under serious advisement

if this f__ing [floundering] body has its f___ing [finalizing] way
will it be coincidence I wonder if some day
our f___-___ing [freedom-loving] patriots
will be forever prevented from legally proclaiming
those brave f___ing [fighting] words:

we are f___ing being f___ed!

From Wikepedia:

Acoustic Kitty was a CIA project launched by the Directorate of Science & Technology in the 1960s attempting to use cats in spy missions. A battery and a microphone were implanted into a cat and an antenna into its tail. Due to problems with distraction, the cat's sense of hunger had to be removed in another operation. Surgical and training expenses are thought to have amounted to over $20 million.

The first cat mission was eavesdropping on two men in a park outside the Soviet compound on Wisconsin Avenue in Washington, D.C.. The cat was released nearby, but was hit and killed by a taxi almost immediately. Shortly thereafter the project was considered a failure and declared to be a total loss.

acoustic kitty
or, **insanity of the surgically-self-altered**

on first reading I laugh uncontrollably
until the choking sounds become sobs
so deep my body wracks in breathless convulsion

I cannot understand how I can cry so
for one surgically Frankensteined cat from forty years ago
that died in such fortunate accident
when today millions starve thousands cry in tortured pain
before my unseeing eye my deaf ear my frozen heart

I think I know I feel I am insane

I understand now, mein Herrn
I know you, meinen Frauen
I am in your shoes, meine Deutsche Schwestern, Brudern.

in my bubble of studied innocence
I tend my beautiful roses
teach and tease my children
scrub my floors pay my bills
am grateful for my good life
carry out my duties as you must have done
back then
today I share pasta, farmer's market salad

and fine swiss chocolate with my musical friends
at the table we hope is safe for now
while we speak in whispered disbelief
of Gitmo and Project Bluebird, Blackwater
        and Manchurian candidate
things done in the shadows in our name
in unmarked buildings across the sea down the street
down the decades
our careful words weaving their trepidacious way
among the wineglasses
we joke about our emails under others' eyes
our tapped conversations saved
certain we are on a list in a somewhere file
we wonder if you had these conversations too
and chuckling our nervousness away
hope the midnight spotlight shines not on us next

my shame is deeper than my soul can bear
my unintact skin cannot afford the luxury of outrage
while my heart threatens to explode from the joy
of Bianconi wrapping us in Chopin lace and longing
our silence holds hostage the unheard rumble of global cruelties
kept warm and thriving in blankets of avoidance:
when was my hunger for something ... what?
... also surgically removed?

I forgive you, my sisters in apathy
I understand you, my fellow citizens in fear
I too breathe the daily sigh of relief
that I am still here to do my unthinking daily chores

we live on faulted lands, my friends
and there is shiver under our feet from time to time
and I understand you across the decades, mein Herrn
and I forgive you, meine Schwestern
as I cannot forgive myself

for I know in that pocket of sanity where truth resides
that here now in 2008 US of A
I am a surgically-self-altered cat
carting implants not of my soul's nature
ich bin ein Berliner of 1933 compliance
my last hope: that the merciful taxi cometh

bending time: memory and clairvoyance

I bend time to remember:
men in chains
	for their brawn alone
women set afire
	for their men's misdeeds
tribes slaughtered
	with divine excuse
cities blown to powder
	for the crude in their veins

I bend time to foresee:
newborns tested
	for pre-existing conditions
cyber-formulas of life-value charts
	for rationing medical care
lab tests to determine
	if her body shut out the legitimate rape
birth and death by jury
war by arcade
peace museums storing relics
	like music	and poetry

past and future so alike
there is no time

talking about trees

. . . in times like these, to have you listen at all, it's necessary to talk about trees.—Adrienne Rich (1929–2012)

yes, let's talk about trees

sturdy old oak that once gave us shade
modeled stability with its long years
has turned to stone
mammoth obstacle impossible to
move or remove
though dying at its heart

gentle willow that once danced with the breeze
graceful ballerina of the verdant lakeside
now stripped of green
hanging leafless lifeless
helpless in the smoky tempest

apple pear and walnut
yielded to the grape
sacrificed to the tablemakers
nourish not the child
fed only corn and sugar

kudzu has no shade for our august days
but chokes the swimming holes of our youth

and saltcedar can compromise
only the littered beachheads
of our horizons

yes, Adrienne Rich,
let's talk about trees

peace is hard

how can I be kind to those who stab me in my underbelly?
can you teach me peace?

how do I repel their blows, their ire that wants my death,
and claim I value peace?
can you teach me survival?

where is my compassion for their pain and need
while my life bleeds away?
can you teach me sanity?

how can I feed their ancient hungers
while I slip into death?
can you teach me endurance?

we are all dying

differently

if not together

how shall we live
together?

about peace and patriotism

e-mail exchange with my cousin: 11-04-2005, 2 years into Iraq war

B writes:
I saw a bumper sticker the other day that I would love to have for my car—**"Peace is Patriotic"**. It would be the first time I have ever considered putting such a thing on my car.

I reply:
Go ahead, Cousin, be daring! Join those young Hungarian men who, in 1956, threw stones at the Russian tanks rolling down the Budapest streets because stones were the only ammunition they had.

Last week there was a nation-wide vigil after the 2000th American soldier died in Iraq; I joined the handful of "peaceniks" in our little town who stood holding candles on our town square in common grief. I was not interested in holding a sign or in greeting passing motorists with any message, or in engaging in like-minded conversation with like-minded townsmen; I just wanted to pay tribute. So I began counting by ones, to get a sense of how many 2000 really is. I gave each number its due; I did not count to see how fast I could; I wanted to count as a kind of meditation on each number, one for each life. When this old body got tired, legs and back aching [I am no longer accustomed to standing in one place for an hour], I just thought of how it might have been for #37 or #456 or #785 to die, and my aching seemed to wane. When I reached roughly 500, I began to cry, and couldn't stop; each number became more painful, more senseless. After about an hour, the group decided to call it quits. I had only reached the first thousand, but I needed to go home also. Once there I felt I had to give the other thousand their due, and sat quietly with a candle, counting the rest, about another hour, an unexpectedly powerful meditation. I wondered how anyone who faults me for being an anti-war protester could think I do not support our troops; I grieve them as a mother, as a countryman, as a patriot, one by one by one by one by one...by one.....by one.......by one........

Yes, B, peace is patriotic. Go ahead, be daring.
Love, V

one way or another

we shall each say our farewells
        drink to our mortality
        yours and mine
across a laden table
or a weaponed field
                                one way or another

I stand before you eyes unshaded
I'm in no mood to become a stranger
I hold out my hand
        open palm packing only peace

I have not the heart to be an enemy

I will prepare before you the fruit you bring
and drink with you
        its nectared juices in common toast
if you will join me   in kind

we shall each drink to our mortality
        say our farewells
one way or another
        across a laden table   or a battlefield

it does matters which

Inauguration Day 2009

just as my neighbor's towering tulip tree
stretching over the aging fence
that connects us and separates us
fills my winter-weary eyes with wonder
catches my aging heart's breath

so your youthful yearning
for a new tomorrow
arcs its blossom-filled promises
across our sagging barriers
sending its silent scent
onto the winter-jaded garden
of my patriot dreams
promising
promising
oh please
the flutter of butterfly wings
on my bleeding hearts
my forget-me-nots

Armageddon of stupidity

An educated citizenry is a vital requisite for our survival
as a free people.—paraphrase of Thomas Jefferson, 1816

we have dumbed down
to the lowest common denominator
science-schmience

we are self-blindfolded maidens
being raped by psychopathic charmers
Citi-Chase-Fargo tells me I am special

we revere the weapons
that nightmare us into compliance
can't take away my AK47

we are brainwashed by fear
into protecting those
who hold us hostage
sure, let's give medicare to Aetna

we have been stockholmed
into saving our abusers

we are all Patty Hearst

I'm glad you can laugh on Sundays

for R-P

I'm glad we can laugh on Sundays
when the trials of the Monday-to-Friday grind
stand in bas-relief
against the shining skies of Sunday sanity

I'm glad you can laugh on Sunday
after those high-priced time-management kids
in their silk shirts and Nike shoes
have held their final
endlessly-postponed consultant meetings
and written their thousand-page proposals
on how you and your two
coffee-sopped overworked office-mates
can work more efficiently
in your windowless carrels
on projects designed to save taxpayer money

I'm glad we can laugh on Sundays

it is good to keep the Sabbath

visiting bee

deep in my gut where gratitude naps
I am awakened by the buzz of the bee in my garden
her visits all too seldom these days

my spirit curtseys to her
with the wide sweep worthy of royalty
as I silently get out of her way
and welcome her
watching from the sidelines as she
busily seeks the sweet rewards of her labor
from my buddleia
penstemon
lipstick sage
alyssum

thank you for coming to my garden
I whisper
next time bring your friends and family
and visit my vegetables

little does she know
as she goes about her daily chore
as unglamorous as my mopping my floor
how her presence opens
the window to my wonderment
my endless awe at the trembling balance
that each of our miniscule movements plays
in that epic symphony we call life
on this rough and fragile planet

assisted care for Mother

spring's first rose bursts its
virgin beauty on my eyes
caring not for whom I vote

its thorn pricks my careless
thumb whether I am thief
or theologian

cool waters slake my thirst
rice and bean they fill my belly
sunset washes me in purple
orange glory regardless
which holy book I read
or none

I am of this earth
and will to it return
as are you
and so will you

she has borne us fed us
held us
and we have used her well
and ill

overworked and under-nourished
nearly used up
she needs us now

how dare we ignore her gasping
tearing ourselves asunder
with silly child debate
over her care

our ailing mother deserves the best

let us be not proud or stubborn
let us call in the experts
roll up our sleeves
and remember to love her

word-sounds

what is life without poetry?

before words

in the soft mists before time began
you knew only the sense of things:
the warmth of wet: cradle of fluid
floating you on its currents   your currents
freedom of not knowing whence you came
wither you journey
only freedom   peace   warm wetness
you learned many dances twirls spins
slides jumps indistinguishable from any you-ness
you the dance

movement genius that you were
tethered now somehow to somewhere
you felt how you were pushed pulled
rough   or caught   safe   or scary
you learned love-pats from thumps
you being danced

eons of time   worlds of change
before the music would come
quietly at first   soft shirring sounds
wetness slurring against the skin of your vessel
moving in the swift and whisp'ring currents
that carried you   shielded you
you sounding   resounding
you the music

and around you then, rhythms   textures of sound
soon you learned lullabies from shrieks
love-songs from sirens
you being sounded

for miniscule centuries of time
those ribbons of sensory chiffon
twirled   interwove on the platform of your being
music and dance intercoursing
music-dance   dancemusic
the only language you knew
learned them well and forever

Miss Hanson

when the classes were so small
Miss Hanson had both third and fourth grades in her room
I was glad
I could have her for two whole years

Miss Hanson was plain and shy
like me
and never made fun of anyone

Miss Hanson started a little school newspaper
to put my first poems in

I loved her
Miss Hanson plain and shy
I didn't know why she wasn't married
she was so nice
they said it was because she was plain
but they meant ugly

Sis told me that years later
just after she finished nurse's training
Miss Hanson called her once
said she had cancer
and would Sis take care of her

Sis said *"no"*
'cause she was still too wet behind the ears
to do such a serious job

Miss Hanson just looked sad, Sis said
we don't know whatever happened to Miss Hanson

I'm sorry Miss Hanson never married
how could anyone so nice not have anybody

but I remember I loved Miss Hanson
plain and shy
and still do

mystery guest

muse of my pen, where are you?
when you do come,
          why then?

now a spark:
firefly alighting into my ebony day

now a river:
rushing, running willy-nilly
where you must
mindless of my mindless map

now a shove:
sudden inconvenient push
impelling me to shores
I never dreamt I'd choose

now elusive ghost:
rebel to my will, enemy of intent
refusing to be caught
defying captivity
stranger to cage

never me:
but running through *my* house
pushing through *my* pen
uninvited visitor inhabiting *my* time:

an only sometime lover
always always too soon gone

muse

she is insistent
in her inconsistency

she calls me when I am busy
with other things I call important

if I do not pay attention
she threatens to abandon me
and sometimes does for an endless while

but if I heed her call
leaving interrupted chores I thought necessary
I lose myself
        somewhere I cannot name

I play   I sing
        I dance
                I suffer   I discover

I am assaulted by images   sounds
        word-avalanches and word-droughts

I struggle   I delight   I curse
        I lose time   I sample eternity

write what you know, she says
        ....I write.............
sometimes I don't know what I write
        is what I know
I pretend I made it up

some day
no one will save my careful budget ledgers
but someone may decide to save
        my carefree book of poems
                insisted

the writer's life

what is the life of the seed
but sitting alone
in some kind of dark
often underground

impelled by fire
of unknown origin
to push
to push
somehow
in improvised ways
against boundaries
not of its own making

until
on some air-filled day
          [if graced by good fortune]
all the miracle that had transpired
is plucked
by an innocent hand

and the seed
finally
discovers its sacred destination

word-quilts

the bolt of cloth is nothing if not plain
until you see its promise
you, who take the shears to the fabric
the needle to the quilt
you, too, are poets

cut and baste and rearrange
reunite the elements
with others of its kind
or different
play like the child you were
cavort with texture, pattern, rhythm

until those scraps of color are transformed
whispers of your soul
seeping through the threads
and offered to your progeny beloved
or to the homeless anonymous
to wrap their shivering dreams together
in reunion with their own warm flesh

words are my bolts of color
poems my quilts

let me wrap you in my words
while I listen to your colors

poetry is

poetry is about what it says, and something else too

poetry dresses in bare essentials, is sometimes even a nudist

poetry plays with the shapes of words, rolls them around,
re-stacks them

poetry wakens the senses: taps our tongues into the singing,
strokes our fingers into the folds,
points our lens toward the vision

poetry gives new wings to words wounded in mid-flight

poetry is the honey helping the medicine go down

poetry revives the tired thought with fresh plasma of language

poetry plays matchmaker for lonely souls in solitary confinement

poetry takes license with facts to get closer to truth

poetry captures the wild things to free them

poetry frames the familiar freshly, paints the new so we can
savor it

poetry vanquishes cliché with rapier, tickles the pedant's foot
with wit's feather

poetry is the magic that delights, surprises, makes broccoli
taste like dessert

poetry says *here is what you have not yet been able to say*

dream-muse

who was he?
this youth with auburn ringlets
framing his quiet knowing eyes
standing like a god
above her sad and wilted body

gently bending to her
his warm hands cupped the cold soles of her feet
how did he know the perfection of that?

warmth rising in her bones
in silence and sightlessness
without caution she rose
embraced him totally
holding him closer than skin

in matching clutch
he gave her everything
whole and strong
losing nothing

as in a dream of sleep
she traced her embrace down his long body
slid like a shedding skin
down his slim legs standing firm

long she laid in fetal knot
around his feet
until in perfect time
like the last sigh of summer
he disappeared unnoticed

night arrived
blessing her waiting darkness
her coiled unknowing patience

finally   fully refilled
she unfolded herself
rose again   whole   safe
in her prized and sufficient   aloneness

poetry readings

across divisions of gender age or shade of skin
beyond banners of political stance
above religious belief
        or spiritual practice
transcending measures of lifestyle
        material comfort
                cultural conditioning

we are brought together here
by a common calling:
        the siren song of the muse
by a common seeking:
        the search for the perfect word

by that which defies all gravity
all merely man-made law:

        the cellular urgency of art

faceless and fameless

poets don't get famous
we just live and die in the cracks
holding the shards of the universe
together
with the grout-blood of
our words

the best we can hope for
some day someone reads us and says
wish I knew him when he lived
not realizing it's now

orphan child

after hearing Mary Oliver read

poetry
orphan child of the arts
avoided when not invisible
begs on public corners
to the deaf lend me your ears
to the blind your eyes
and penniless
uninvited
saunters home
to the silence of dimly lit stars
the solace of dawning sun
the company of breeze and birdsong
honey on the hungry tongue

two haiku about a neighbor's cat

cat watches lizard
I watch cat watching lizard
sun watches us all

bird on high branch trills
fish at pond's surface nibble
cat on fence ponders

gardener poet

for Stanley Kunitz

in that place where primal need meets word

there
seed is planted in rich loam of pain and desire

there
in language of longing
does hope of fruit await
in sacred secret cells of creation

there
under soft rains of care
and labored devotion to birthing
comes forth the tender sprout

there
swathed in perfect mystery
does the unsteady stalk sturdy itself
and reach for light
for air
for free and open space

there
does the grunting tongue finally refine itself
to lay its kiss
a garden garland
upon the brow of the beloved

fine wine
is like
bottled
poetry
let us
share
a sip
or two
or like
tipsy lovers
quaff a carafe
til heart's awhirl
on the love and
the swirl of delicate
tastes on the tongue

joyful noises

love, music, mortality, and other vibrations

love is

love, not at all blind
is the perceptive eye
that knows what to see, what not

love knows the difference
between gifts
pay-backs
and bribes

love cares when it should
does not when it matters
knows when to push
when to wait

love spreads the balm of forgiveness
on the guilt-scraped skin
of imperfection

love hums silently when others grieve
joins in when they carol

like a warm furry dog
love sleeps undisturbed on the feet
of the wordless long-joined couple

love blesses the lover
who blesses the beloved

miracles

Here I sit at my computer on 11-11-11, reading hours of emails and petitions and forwards about Delaware River fracking, and Mississippi's rejection of personhood for women's eggs, and move-your-money-day, and tar sands pipelines, and constitutional amendments to limit campaign funds, and Occupy Oakland's massive challenge to stay non-violent in this most violence-racked city, and polar bears without ice floes, and torture of lesbians in Ecuador, and, and,............and I am overcome with gratitude:

.... to Hippocrates and Hahnemann and Curie and Pasteur and Salk and my Dr. Michael and Debbie and herb gardens and bees and sunshine and rain and the loyalty of seed, for helping me be here still, octogenarian on fire

.... to my parents and grandparents and their ancestors for their good genes and their good sense to cross the daunting Atlantic to labor in coal mines and cigar factories to make me, to make me better, to make me a better life

.... to Ben Franklin and Tom Edison and Singer and to my furnace for keeping me warm, and to all the other comforting and safety-making inventions in this shelter where I can close my eyes in sleep unafraid

.... to those who created language out of grunts, and Gutenberg, and my Dad who taught me to read while tending to my sixth-year chickenpox, and to Miss Hanson who liked my third-grade poems, and to those colonials who created Rutgers University without ever having me in mind

.... to a lifetime of listening wonderment for the Mozart melodies that reside in my head, my brain's personal MP3 downloads

.... to Susan and the other suffragettes who marched and suffered nights in jail for my right to be a woman voting, though they never knew me personally

.... to Ghandi and MLK and Mother Theresa and Eleanor Roosevelt and the Friends and COs and Occupy-all, all those who hold the light

.... to the power of those who loved me and love me still, and by so doing keep me whole still, whether they walk the earth or no longer grace it

.... to whatever mysteries keep my mind alert and capable of outrage, keep my soul alive and capable of gratitude

.... to my diaphragm that keeps me breathing, I know not why

thanks for the invite

for Doug Stout, once long ago

you asked me over
I'm on my way

but don't do anything fun
before I get there

I want to enter a room dragged in grey
trail in merriment and josh
scatter popcorns of laughter
splatter Pollocks of color in my wake
and when I leave
have you beg me take the leftovers home

so thanks for the invite
I'm on my way

don't do anything fun
before I get there

music manuscripts

scouting the museum anterooms
I find the exhibit I came to see
music manuscripts writ in their very hand
Beethoven Chopin Mozart
sheets of paper left behind
beyond the flesh that once fashioned phrases
channeled direct from soul's ear to fingertip
to pen to paper that we might hear
what came to them original

here is more than music
here is the body's dance
the rush of life revealing what the melody cannot
betraying daily habit pattern character

Chopin's notes precisely patterned
like tatted lace on page
delicately set out, neat, exact
as unblemished as a Victorian bosom
clothed with fragile embellishment
transparently revealing all

Beethoven's pages betraying brashness
spattered with stain coffee tears blood
impatient ink spots forced by inspiration
vulgar power exposing a brutal beauty
and secret senses pulsed and pushed
to unabashed immortality
as if to outpace the coming silence

and there, **Mozart's** strokes
slanting forward like a lithe and limber runner
darting among the melodies
rapid sure and confident
scribing a master faster than himself
the final note in sight of the first
the course known from the beginning
the flesh unable to outrun time
the music flashing through eternity

Gershwin concerto in F

the City at 4 am
        finally left alone

by-day-shiny skyscrapers
        now grey ghosts
        dripping dirty day-sweat
with nothing to do but hang around
        bleary-eyed

sleepy streets with blood-shot lids
        huddle round the littered sidewalks
        against the chill of night
abandoned lights drowsily blink their weariness
        to no one watching

no movement but the slow shuffle
        of those ending the night late
        or starting the day early
                all the same

low hum
slow pulse of barely breathing

needing oh so needing just a couple hours sleep
        before the all-too-soon beloved frenzy
                begins again

solo recital

for Jeffrey Kahane

he seats himself at the piano
lowers his head for a silent moment
as if entering a secret chamber through a low portal
places his velvet iron fingers on the keys
eases into the music
then sends it forth to
        reach us
        teach us
        touch us
the many hundreds of us in concert
on nerve endings we had not known
our souls have

for Chester Aaron at 90

the now faint still sacred visages of Dachau
visited upon your barely begun man-years
trail in your wake
not like scent of old lavender
around our great-grandmothers
but whiffs of acrid smokestack
poisoning the fresh morning fog

as if by warlock wisdom
you have warded off their evil
with garlands of garlic
gracing your grounds
your years
your nighttime visitors

naughty fifth-grade glint
still glistening in your eye
step now into your tenth decade
dear friend
surrounded by your own tomes
of fact and fiction and fancy
lively lyrics still alighting on page
spewed forth from your mighty imagination
that dances still with memories
of life and death

while we
this musical chorale
of admiration and delight
embrace you now
gold and grunge alike
kaleidoscopic past
Maytime present
and all the future your irreverent gods
will allow

Rift Valley, Kenya, August 1989

as the last purple light of western dusk fades to black
here on the south rim of this vast African valley
I sit on the edge of the wide night
watching it spread slowly and endlessly before me

no light but numberless stars
sprinkled randomly above
defying gravity
teasing the great dark with silver sparkle
as if to deny its dominion

silence as large as the onyx sky
settles its blanket gently
on the drowsy earth
and peace lulls the beast in me
as well as in the lioness
opens its arms to the listening soul

I feel the valley in my bones
I am in its skin
in its pristine wilderness
its rough unhurried tests of life
its primaeval unsentimental innocence

from this unspoiled valley of original birth
this vast enveloping ebony womb
this sweeping swath of possibility
I hear maternal grunts of my mother Lucy
primal mother of us all
echo through the eons
past parades of civilizations
giving birth to us all
giving me life

reunited with my mother
I hear her soft primate lullaby
waft on the low valley breezes
I am in the original cradle
I know all who ever lived and ever will
as kin as family

requiem for Michael Jackson

poor little rich boy
poor little lonely prince
on this jumbled journey
this unquiet odyssey of the flesh
how many masks have you donned
by force of light
by dint of darkness
ebony shadows of your beleaguered
radiant soul

in that somewhere sometime ether
before being birthed into this earthly form
were you asked?
were you sent?
despite the demons of imperfect flesh
so dauntless and so drear
you seemed to know so soon your path
so sure the golden gift
so well the message clear

spot-lighted pedestal for backyard playground
eternal child made manifest
on the only stage you knew
Disney-ized dreams of childhood
found only in the Alice-y wonderlands
of others' altered states
in your sequin-covered innocence
you architected in luxurious desperation
on this rich earth and in your fanciful mind
the never-never-landscapes
you mistook for sanctuary

how many castles had you built
and never found a home

how many dazzling glories
gilded trinkets
midnight saunters
sharks and shielders
failed the promises you sought
in their heavy cost

in how many beds on how many jaunts
around this earthen spaceship
had restful slumber fled your restless mind
before that last blessed peace
vein-dripped and silent
arrived too soon
and unannounced

float now, radiant soul,
in that shadowless state of painless light
the real eternal childhood
and rest apiece before your next appearance
you rehearsed this life away for
to pursue
perhaps
the perfect
persuasive
performance

after the goodbye

for Rachel

on the kitchen counter
last memento of your visit
anticipated so long   lived too short
your favorite mug sits abandoned
hastily half-emptied before your pre-dawn leaving
too early for my liking
I should rinse it out, put it away

beside it
untouched in the pyrex coffee-maker
hauled out of hiding for your use
last inch of now cold coal-colored brew
echoes the darkness behind my eyes
no coffee drinker I, I cannot throw it out

in my writing-room-turned-guest-room
rumple-sheeted bed
bare closet hangers   cleaned-out drawers
empty wineglass from last night's nightcap
stand silent witness   to a quiet too large
for my emptied heart to re-embrace

I want to erase the aching by tearing off those sheets
laundering out the looming loneliness
putting it all back together in neat guest-ready primness

no, I want instead to leave it like this forever
to keep reminders of the life in me re-awakened
by the vim the vigor the liveliness
you brought to these rooms

how could you tear up my habit-rutted daily schedule
and leave me only days later
my spirit left to deal with the joyful debris
even while bass-note thrum-beats signal the coming dusk

but please
come again   soon

the seven stages of aging

1. maturity

2. AARP

3. active senior

4. elder

5. "you look great!"

6. elderly

7. "just looks asleep"

my body my abode

this house I moved into
at outset seeming younger than I
has served me well:
sturdy of foundation   solid of beam
slant of structure barely noticeable
small flaws here and there
on the whole sound enough
to shelter me passing well
and last a lifetime

now and then   especially early on
distracted by temptations   obligations
obsessions without
I neglected its upkeep   forgot its maintenance
allowed silent mustinesses to take hold
interlopers that sleep in darkened
caverns of permanent night
left unexamined in the busi-ness
of that inattention we call life
such lapses in my youth and prime
mattered little at the time

every so often burst pipe burnt-out circuit
unexpected injury
reveal flaws of form or function
requiring more than cosmetic fix
reminding me how vital my attention
to seeing to this house I live in

no matter the impatient will that pulls me out of doors
or urge to play on instruments of the world
demands of aging structure
make daily care a more vital chore
the longer I have been here
the more urgent that necessity

yet it remains my home
the place at end of day
I find myself ensconced comfy or not
and despite inevitable change
grateful for the familiar

some day
regardless of entreaty or resistance
I will find this old place
uninhabitable

time will evict me one way or another
peaceably I hope
leaving behind all:
all souvenirs   all promises
all sins omissions and debris

allowing me perhaps
only a trace of nostalgia
and one iota of relief

See YouTube video of the author at the Healdsburg
Literary Guild's 2012 Graveside Reading.avi
(http://www.youtube.com/watch?v=91YbRO6QL3s&feature=plcp)

after the funeral

no use denying it
this is how I know it will happen

after I finally leave this house I live in
the one whose basic bones were sound enough
the one I maintained passing well I thought
but not so well I couldn't enjoy it
this my earthly home my shelt'ring playground

but when it becomes as it must some day
uninhabitable
so I will have to leave behind
its faults and failings

this is what I know you will do
you will go through my things
looking for leftovers of my spirit
to remember me by
little forget-me-not *tchotchkies*
to remind you who I was

you will pore over the family albums
and guess what year those photos were taken
and what you were doing then
and who those other strangers were

and then
I know it surely as I write these words
then
and perhaps then for the first time
you will read the poems I sent you long ago
the ones in the dusty little books
on unvisited shelves of your earthly home
you will scan the family stories I wrote and sent you
seeking like panners of old
for nuggets of gold with your name inscribed
and you will say
oh yeah, but I don't remember it that way

you will watch the home movies you took back when
and rerun the scenes that caught me unaware
and laugh

and wonder what is on that DVD I sent you
after I became that laureate thing
enough to finally watch it

and when you come across the videos
marked *"training"*
your curiosity may introduce you finally
to the me you never knew
the one who got degrees
and spent her decades
helping strangers find their way
and in her maturehood
taught her students some of what she'd learned

and then perhaps
you'll wonder why you never asked
about my work
about my self
why you didn't read my poems
my stories when I sent them

and you might think of a hundred questions
you'd ask me if only I weren't gone
darn it

About the Author

Vilma Olsvary Ginzberg was the fifth Healdsburg [CA] Literary Laureate [2008/2009].

Active in the Healdsburg Literary Guild for over a decade, she hosted the Guild's monthly Third Sunday Salon 2007-2012.

A retired psychologist, she turned to writing in earnest late in life, and since 2004 has published four books of poetry: *Colors of Glass* in 2004, *Murmurs & Outcries* in 2007, *Snake Pit* in 2010, and *I Don't Know How to Do This, poems on aging,* in 2011, which is also in DVD and CD form. In addition, she was co-editor, with Doug Stout, of the anthology *Present at the Creation,* 2006, a publication of the Healdsburg Literary Guild.

Her work has appeared in anthologies: *Present at the Creation,* 2006, *A Day in the Life of Healdsburg,* 2007, *Sometimes in the Open,* 2009, *When the Muse Calls,* 2009, and *Continent of Light,* 2011. One of her family stories, *The Christmas Lesson,* was dramatized by The Imaginists theater group in 2007. A video of her reading of one of her poems, *Ask Any Woman,* was part of a SlaughterhouseSpace multimedia art installation in 2008.

DVDs of each of her 2008 and 2009 Laureate readings are available.

She has completed the first volume of her memoirs, *When the Iris Blooms,* and continues writing the second, *Mostly Roses.*

She is proud to be an active poet with the 100 Thousand Poets for Change, www.100thousandpoetsforchange.com.

For more information, contact vilmaginz@aol.com.

www.ingramcontent.com/pod-product-compliance
Lightning Source LLC
LaVergne TN
LVHW050543100826
845148LV00002B/657
* 9 7 8 0 9 8 3 8 8 9 2 7 4 *